Divine
APPOINTMENTS

Allen Domelle

Visit our website at:
Oldpathsjournal.com
For more copies write:
Allen Domelle Ministries
PO Box 1595
Bethany, OK 73008
903.746.9632

TABLE OF CONTENTS

When It All Started

It all started when I was seven years old. We were living with my aunt, Bessie Parr, and she had a great passion for teaching her nephew how to lead people to Jesus Christ. She bought me a pocket-sized New Testament and sat me down to show me how to lead someone to Jesus Christ.

She got a pen and underlined the verses that she felt would be the easiest verses to use to tell others how to be saved at a young age. Beside each verse, she wrote the next verse where I was to go when I was done explaining the verse. She went verse-by-verse through the Roman's Road and taught me what to tell a person about each verse.

After she was done teaching me how to lead someone to Christ, she then practiced with me several days in a row. One day she told me that she wanted to take me soul winning. She brought me to the park across the street from her house, and we were able to see a couple of people saved. It was very exciting to see people get saved. She told me that God could use me to tell anyone how to get saved if I would just ask them about their eternity.

It was a couple of days later when I was playing with my friend that the Holy Spirit moved on my heart to talk to him about getting saved. Yes, God can use a 7-year-old boy to tell people how to go to Heaven. I was a little nervous because I didn't want to lose my friend, but with every bit of courage I could muster, I asked him if he were to die if he knew 100% that he would go to Heaven. To my shock, he said he did not know. I pulled that little New Testament out of the back pocket of my jeans and brought him through the Romans Road. When I was done presenting the Gospel, I asked him if he wanted to get saved. That afternoon, my friend bowed his head and received Jesus Christ as his personal Saviour.

That is where it all started. It has been over four decades, and I am still telling people how to go to Heaven. From the time that I told my friend how to get saved to this day, I have seen thousands of people accept Christ as their Saviour. It has been an amazing ride, and the ride won't be done until my feet step onto the shores of Heaven.

I must tell you that I don't consider myself the greatest soul winner. I'm just like you; there are still times when I become apprehensive about asking someone about their salvation. There are times when I have to motivate myself to fulfill my responsibility to tell others the Gospel. I understand that there are many better soul winners than myself, but I also understand that God doesn't need me or you to be the best soul winner; He simply needs us to be a tool that He can use to tell others how to get saved.

Daniel 12:3 says, *"And they that be wise shall shine as the brightness of the firmament; and they that turn many to righteousness as the stars for ever and ever."* Many will never know my Aunt Bessie, but she will be rewarded for taking the time to teach me how to be a soul winner. She was a wise lady who realized that the more people I led to Christ, the brighter my light would shine.

My friend, the purpose of writing this manuscript is to give you the tools you need to become a soul winner. The darker this world becomes because of sin, the more we need Christians to let their light brightly shine. The only way your light will get brighter is by turning others to righteousness through Jesus Christ. When you learn how to lead people to Christ, you will start a journey that leads to great joy, and it will help you to lay up treasures in Heaven. There are thousands of people whom God will lead across your path during your lifetime whom you could show how to get saved.

Over the next pages of this manuscript, I am going to use the story of Philip and the Ethiopian eunuch to show you the importance of divine appointments. There are thousands of divine appointments God has scheduled for you, just like He had for me on that day when I led my first person to Jesus Christ. I don't claim to be an expert in the area of soul winning, but I do know the One who will daily help you to see people saved if you will answer your divine appointment.

Going to the Desert

The early church was experiencing great persecution. Saul was creating *"havock of the church"* by *"entering into every house, and haling men and women"* and committing them to prison. (Acts 8:3) The Christians scattered to avoid the persecution, but everywhere they went they were *"preaching the word."* (Acts 8:4)

Philip was one of the people who left Jerusalem. Acts 8:5 says, *"Then Philip went down to the city of Samaria, and preached Christ unto them."* As he preached this revival meeting, God worked in the hearts of the people of that city, and many souls were saved. It was a miraculous revival! The Scriptures tell us that those who were possessed with unclean spirits were freed from their control. Many of the sick were healed. The result of this revival are seen in Acts 8:8 when it says, *"And there was great joy in that city."*

The revival didn't stop there. There was a man who was a sorcerer in Samaria who's name was Simon. A sorcerer is similar to a witch doctor. If you know anything about witch doctors, they control the city or village where they live. When Simon saw those whom he had *"bewitched"* living a happy life, he knew he needed what they had. After hearing Philip preach about Jesus Christ, this man also got saved. Wow, what a revival meeting!

The story changes here with an unseemly command by an angel of the LORD. In the middle of this revival meeting, this angel commanded Philip to *"Arise, and go toward the south unto the way that goeth down from Jerusalem unto Gaza, which is desert."* (Acts 8:26) This was a strange command because the city was experiencing change because of the revival meeting, but his obedience led to a divine appointment that every Christian can only wish they could experience.

I can see Philip walking in the desert wondering why God would want him to leave that great revival just to go to the desert where there would be nobody to whom he could talk. I'll be honest with you; I don't know that I could have done what Philip did. I've been in deserts, and there is nothing there. However, Philip completely understood the principle of Proverbs 3:5-6 which says, *"Trust in the LORD with all thine heart; and lean not unto thine own understanding. In all thy ways acknowledge him, and he shall direct thy paths."* He understood that God wouldn't give such a command without a purpose.

What Philip didn't know was that God was already working on the heart of someone who could be used to reach his country for Christ. There was a man of Ethiopia, a eunuch who served under Candace the queen, who was returning from worshipping in Jerusalem. This man was searching for answers, but he didn't find any in the service he attended.

This eunuch had apparently stopped his chariot in the middle of the desert to read the Scriptures. He happened to be reading from Isaiah 53. The Spirit of God told Philip to join this man. As Philip drew near, he heard him reading from the very passage of Scripture that talked about Jesus' sacrificial death on the cross.

Philip asked the eunuch in verse 30, *"Understandest thou what thou readest?"* This man said in the next verse, *"How can I, except some man should guide me?"* Philip quickly got into the chariot and began to explain to him what that Scripture was all about. The eunuch asked Philip when they came to some water, *"See, here is water; what doth hinder me to be baptized?"* (Acts 8:36) It was here that Philip explained that if he believed with *"all his heart,"* he could get baptized. Philip was making it clear that baptism couldn't save him, only Jesus could save. The eunuch responded by saying, *"I believe that Jesus Christ is the Son of God."* My friend, this is salvation. History teaches that this eunuch went back to his country and reached it for Jesus Christ.

It was not a coincidence that this man was reading the very passage of Old Testament Scripture that talked about Jesus' sacrificial death. It was no accident that this man was coming back from a religious service, and was still searching for an answer. It was not a coincidence that Philip happened to be in the desert. This, my friend, is a divine appointment.

Let me remind you that God is not finished scheduling divine appointments; He has plenty of them for you if you will be as sensitive to the voice of the Holy Spirit as was Philip. I don't know where your *"desert"* will be, but I can promise you there are plenty of them that you come across every day. Your *"desert"* may be at the restaurant, grocery store, gas station or park. Your *"desert"* may be when you pass someone as you walk down the sidewalk, or it could be that business appointment you have with someone. I don't know where your *"desert"* will happen, but I know the LORD has one for you. You don't have to wish you can have a divine appointment like Philip, because God has many scheduled for you as well.

It's a Soul

My daughter and I were taking a flight from Dallas to Pittsburgh for a revival meeting. God was kind to us and allowed us to be bumped up to first class. We were sitting in the front row of first class, when the gate agent entered the plane, poked her head into the cockpit and said, "There are 140 souls on this vessel."

When I heard her say that there were 140 souls, I leaned over to my daughter and said, "Did you hear that?" She said, "Hear what?" I said, "Did you hear what the gate agent just said?" She told me that she didn't hear what she said. I told my daughter what was said, but it didn't hit my daughter the same way that it hit me. I told her that the gate agent didn't say there were 140 people aboard, but she said there were 140 souls on the vessel.

This is one of the secrets that will help you to become bold in your soul winning. You see, there is a soul behind the facade of flesh that we see. That soul never dies. That soul that you can't see will either go to a real Heaven or a real Hell. If that soul is not saved, it will go to a real Hell that has a literal fire, *"Where their worm dieth not, and the fire is not quenched."* (Mark 9:44) When you realize what you see is a soul-clothed body, you will find it much easier to tell people about Jesus Christ.

When you start seeing people through the eyes of Jesus, you will see there is a soul that lives forever. When you see people as souls, you won't see the color of their skin or the physical stature of their body. When you see people as souls, you won't see the tattoos on their body or the gauges in their ears. When you see people as souls, you won't see the diamond rings or the fancy suits they wear. When you see people as souls, you won't see them as poor, rich or middle class. When you see people as souls, you won't see how much they have or have not accomplished; you will only see a soul. When you see people as souls, you won't see their titles or status. When you see people as souls, you will constantly be reminded that their soul will either go to Heaven or Hell.

My friend, I don't know what the population of your city is, but let me remind you that the population only represents how many souls that will either go to Heaven or Hell. You will only reach those souls if you will *"Arise, and go..."* like Philip did.

You will never find your divine appointment until you *"Arise and go."* There is someone whom God is working on today whom you could reach if you will simply *"Arise and go."* When you start seeing people as a soul, you will find that *"Arise and go"* won't be as difficult as you think.

Let me remind you of Luke 19:10 which says, *"For the Son of man is come to seek and to save that which was lost."* Jesus didn't come seeking to win the church softball league, but He came seeking souls. Jesus didn't come seeking to make wealth, but He came to seek souls. Jesus didn't come seeking political position, but He came seeking souls. Jesus didn't come seeking to build a successful business, but He came to seek souls.

My friend, God doesn't give awards for winning the church sports league, but He does reward the Christian for every soul that they lead to Him. There is nothing wrong with making money, building a successful business, enjoying a hobby, or building a fancy house, but in the end that will not matter if a soul goes to Hell.

Someone said to me, "I wish I could have the soul winning experiences that you have." My answer to that statement is, "*Arise, and go.*" There are plenty of divine appointments scheduled for you, but you are going to have to go if you want to find them. You are going to have to look beyond the facade that a person has on the outside and see their soul. I promise you will discover it won't be that difficult to find your divine appointment if you see people as souls, and simply enquire as to where their soul will spend an eternity when they die.

The Inconvenience of Divine Appointments

Divine appointments are obvious, yet they're not. They can be as obvious as one person sitting in a chariot in the middle of the desert if you will simply slow down and open your eyes. Imagine if Philip's sole focus was on going to the desert, he would have missed the Ethiopian eunuch and his divine appointment.

One thing I have learned about divine appointments is they never happen at the most opportune times or in the most convenient places. You will find that most divine appointments will be an inconvenience from what you are doing or where you are going. It was not a convenient place for Philip to go soul winning because he had to go to the *"desert"* for this divine appointment to happen. It also was not an opportune time for this divine appointment, because he was in the middle of a great revival meeting. However, he was willing to be inconvenienced, and his willingness led to a divine appointment that we regularly read about and quote in our lessons and sermons.

I was preaching in Berne, Indiana. It was a Sunday morning, and the hotel I was staying in only had cereal for their breakfast items. I am not a cereal lover, so I decided to go down the street to the local McDonalds to get some scrambled eggs and sausage. I didn't have too much time because I was to teach Sunday school that morning.

On my way out of the hotel, as I was walking to the van, I passed a man who was sitting on a bench talking on his cell phone. The Holy Spirit told me to stop and talk to him, but my excuse to the Holy Spirit was that I needed to hurry because I needed to eat my breakfast and go to Sunday school. I proceeded on my way to go to McDonalds, completely ignoring the Holy Spirit's prodding. I ordered my food, sat down and ate it, and drank a whole cup of coffee before I headed back to the hotel.

Once I arrived back at the hotel, I noticed that the man who was on his phone was still sitting there on the bench. The Holy Spirit said to me, "I kept him here for you, what are you going to do?" Again, I was focused on trying to get ready to go to Sunday school. As I was purposely passing this man to go back to my room, he said to me, "It sure is a beautiful day, isn't it?" At that point, I knew I had to stop.

I chatted a bit about what he was doing in town and then reached into my pocket to give him my personal tract. I said after I gave him the tract, "By the way, on the back of that card you will find a message on how you can go to Heaven." He turned the tract over and looked at it which prodded me to say, "Sir, have you ever thought about going to Heaven?" I asked Him, "If you died right now, are you 100% sure that you would go to Heaven?" He said, "You know, I just retired a couple months ago. I have been wondering where I would go if I died." I asked him if I could sit next to him and show him from the Scriptures how he could go to Heaven. In just a few minutes, Kenneth bowed his head and prayed to received Christ as his personal Saviour.

It was certainly not a convenient time or place for me to witness to Kenneth, but had I not interrupted my purpose to get ready for Sunday school, I would have missed that divine appointment. Kenneth would have never heard the precious Gospel of Jesus Christ had I not been willing to be inconvenienced. No, it wasn't an opportune time or a convenient place, but it was the right time and place for Kenneth to get saved.

If you are like me, I can get so focused on what I am doing and where I am going that I miss who the LORD is sending across my path. My friend, God has many divine appointments scheduled, but you are going to have to slow down and open your eyes to see those divine appointments who are ready to hear the Gospel. You are going to have to be willing to be inconvenienced if you want to find your divine appointment. Divine appointments are all around you if you will just slow down and look.

If the only time you look for divine appointments is during the scheduled soul-winning time, you are going to miss hundreds of them that God has planned for you. I'm not saying that you won't have divine appointments during the scheduled soul-winning time, but I am saying that many divine appointments are awaiting you if you are willing to be inconvenienced. My friend, slow down and don't get so focused that you miss those like Kenneth who are waiting for you to tell them the Gospel. Trust me, they are there, you just have to look. If you will slow down and look, you will find that they are as obvious as a man sitting in his chariot in the desert.

Listening for the Tug

Philip would have never realized his divine appointment had he not listened to the Holy Spirit. Acts 8:29 says, *"Then the Spirit said unto Philip, Go near, and join thyself to this chariot."* The Spirit of God is as interested in souls getting saved as is the Son of God. The Spirit of God is the part of the Godhead that will lead you to your divine appointments if you will listen for the tug in your heart.

Imagine if Philip was like the average Christian who felt the tug of the Holy Spirit's voice, but ignored it because it wasn't convenient, or it wasn't the right time. If he had ignored the Holy Spirit's voice, the eunuch would have never been saved, and Ethiopia would have never been reached with the Gospel. The biggest reason this world has not been reached with the Gospel is because many Christians haven't listened to the tug on the heart by the Holy Spirit to talk to an individual who will go to some place where nobody else would go and reach with the Gospel. It truly comes down to listening to the Holy Spirit.

It was a Monday morning, and I wanted to go and get a cup of coffee from a Starbucks that was not far from the hotel. I was preaching a revival meeting in Virginia, and I had some time that morning to get some work done. As I passed the front desk on my way to get a cup of coffee, I greeted the hotel clerk behind the front desk. It only took about fifteen minutes to get the cup of coffee and get back to my room to start working on a sermon I felt I needed to preach that night.

While I was working on the sermon, the Holy Spirit told me that I needed to stop working on the sermon and go talk to the hotel clerk at the front desk about Christ. I reminded the Holy Spirit that I was studying for a sermon, and that I needed that time to prepare for the services that night. The Holy Spirit then reminded me that He was very capable of helping me preach that night, but that He wanted me to go talk to the clerk. After a few back and forth's with the Holy Spirit, I told Him that if I messed up that night that it was His fault. It wasn't that I didn't want to tell the hotel clerk how to go to Heaven, it was just that I'm a focused individual who does one thing at a time. Leaving what I was doing wouldn't "fit" into my schedule for studying, but it "fit" into the Holy Spirit's schedule for someone to hear the Gospel.

I obeyed and went to the front desk and handed a tract to the hotel clerk. I invited her to come and hear me preach that week while I was in the revival. She asked me what church I was preaching at, and I told her that I was preaching at the Baptist church in town. She then told me that she was a Catholic, but her husband would probably enjoy coming because he was a Baptist. As my usual humor is, I responded to her by saying, "I bet that makes for an interesting marriage." We both laughed at the statement, but then I asked about her nationality. I had a suspicion what it was, but I wanted to confirm it before I put my foot in my mouth. She told me she was a Filipino. I then asked her if she was born in the Philippines or the States. She said she was born in the States, but that her mother was born in the Philippines. I asked her where her mother was born, and she told me I probably wouldn't know the city. I asked her to try me; so she told me that her mother was born in Iloilo, Philippines. "I know where that is," I responded. I told her that I had preached there many times and that my father-in-law was a missionary about an hour from there.

That small conversation led to me being able to show Yvonne how to get saved, and her accepting Christ as Saviour. This would not have happened had I not listened to the tug of the Holy Spirit telling me to leave my room to go talk to her about her salvation. It was a divine appointment arranged by the Holy Spirit that an evangelist from Texas would meet up with a hotel clerk whose mother was born in a city where I had preached, which opened the door for her to get saved.

My friend, the Holy Spirit will lead you to those divine appointments if you will just listen to the tug on your heart. You should ask the Holy Spirit every day to lead you to the person who He is already working on. If you listen to the tug of the Holy Spirit, you will find that He will lead you to those individuals who have something in common with you. If you will listen and obey, you will find divine appointments will be met every week of your life. Let me encourage you to start obeying that little tug on your heart about talking to someone about Christ. The heart that listens for the tug, and the individual who obeys that voice will find exciting appointments of soul-winning experiences that God has in store for them.

Doors Don't Get Saved

One of the biggest mistakes many soul winners make is that they only go house to house to find someone to whom they can show the Gospel. There is nothing wrong with this other than, doors don't get saved. I believe there is value in going house to house, as that is what the Apostle Paul said he did in Acts 20:20; however, you should never solely depend on going to a door to see someone saved.

Acts 8:27-28 says, *"And he arose and went: and, behold, a man of Ethiopia, an eunuch of great authority under Candace queen of the Ethiopians, who had the charge of all her treasure, and had come to Jerusalem for to worship, Was returning, and sitting in his chariot read Esaias the prophet."* You will notice that there was no door for Philip to knock on, only a man sitting in a chariot. If he were only going to look for a door to knock on, he would have missed this great opportunity to lead the Ethiopian eunuch to Christ.

Divine appointments will only be realized if you look for them. There are several instances in the Scriptures, if not most conversions, where people were saved away from their house. The first thing Jesus did after he returned from being tempted by Satan was to walk by the shores of the Sea of Galilee. As He walked by the shores, He saw Peter and Andrew casting their net into the sea. It was at the sea of Galilee that He told them in Matthew 4:19, *"Follow me, and I will make you fishers of men."*

It was after a long day of traveling to a city of Samaria, called Sychar, when Jesus stopped at Jacob's well and met a woman who was living in adultery. Jesus simply asked her in John 4:7, *"Give me to drink."* That statement led to a long dialogue about the woman's spiritual condition, eventually resulting in her accepting Christ as Saviour. Her conversion led to the excitement to go back into the city and tell the people, *"Come, see a man, which told me all things that ever I did: is not this the Christ?"* (John 4:29)

Philip was simply walking through the desert when he came across the eunuch who was searching the Scriptures for an answer. This was no chance; this was a divine appointment. Enough space in this small manuscript could not be given to tell of the countless numbers of salvation conversions that happened as people witnessed to people every day along their way.

You must realize that your divine appointment may be the first person you see today.

I was preaching a revival meeting for a friend in Baton Rouge, Louisiana. When I arrived at the airport, he asked me if I would be willing to make a few visits with him before he took me to the hotel room for the night. Of course, I was thrilled to be able to help him with this request.

We were visiting people in some of the rural areas before he brought me to a trailer park to visit a family he was trying to get to come to church for the revival meeting. After getting into the car to go to our next stop, we were driving out of the trailer park when I told him to stop the car. He put his foot on the brake and asked if something were wrong. I told him some men were standing by their truck that I wanted to invite to church. He parked the car, and I got out to go talk to the men and invited them to church. After I talked with them for a short time, I asked them, "If you died today, are you 100% sure that your past, present and future sins are all paid?" One man told me he was confident and gave me a clear testimony of his salvation. The other man looked at me and said he didn't know. I quickly pulled the New Testament out of my pocket to show him the Gospel, and after a few minutes of explaining the Scriptures, Deven bowed his head and prayed to receive Christ as His Saviour.

The key is looking for people whom God allows to cross your path. I think of a time when I was coming home from the airport when I saw the gas prices at a station seemed to be much lower than normal. I quickly made a u-turn to go back and fill my car up with gas. While I was fueling my car, I noticed a gentleman wearing an Alabama hat. Well, that caught my attention, because I'm a big fan. I said to him what every Alabama fan says to each other, "Roll Tide." We began to talk about the team we had in common, and before long the conversation turned to his eternal destiny and where he would spend it. Alvin graciously stopped what he was doing to hear the greatest news a person could ever hear, and eventually accepted Christ as his Saviour.

I could tell you of hundreds of illustrations where God allowed me to strike up a conversation with someone because of something that I had in common with them. Your personal interests are truly conversation starters if you will use them. It is no mistake that someone crosses your path who has the same interests as you, or has gone through something that you have experienced. These are what we call divine appointments. They are everywhere! The only difference between those who can tell about their divine appointments from those who can't is that those who have experienced them simply kept their eyes open along the path, and used that common interest to talk to someone about Jesus Christ.

If the only time you wait to find divine appointments is when you go to knock on doors for soul winning, you are going to become discouraged by the few that you come across. Let me encourage you the next time you go soul winning to stop and talk to the first person you see. It may be someone who is walking down the street on your way to visit someone. Whenever you see someone who has your same interests, be sure to use that interest as an ice-breaker to start a conversation so you can tell them about Jesus Christ. Your soul-winning experiences will become exciting when you realize that doors don't get saved but people do. Let me encourage you to break out of your comfort zone and talk to people, especially those whom God leads across your path who have the same interests. It is then that you will start finding those divine appointments God has scheduled for you.

DIVINE APPOINTMENTS

No Pressure, You're Just the Delivery Boy

One of the biggest deterrents to people going soul winning is the pressure they put on themselves that they don't want to mess up in giving out the Gospel. I always appreciate their desire to want to be sure to give the Gospel as clearly as they can, but may I tell you that you are not the one who saves people. It is not up to you to make sure people get saved; it is up to you to deliver the message of salvation and let the Holy Spirit do the rest of the work.

Throughout the Scriptures, you will find that God never commands a Christian to save an individual, He only commands that they deliver the Gospel. Acts 1:8 says, *"But ye shall receive power, after that the Holy Ghost is come upon you: and ye shall be witnesses unto me..."* Notice that our job is to be a witness. Mark 16:15 says, *"And he said unto them, Go ye into all the world, and preach the gospel to every creature."* Again, you will notice that the Christian's job is to *"preach the gospel to every creature."* You will always find that God never puts the pressure on the Christian to be sure people get saved, He only commands the Christian to get the Gospel to as many people as they can.

In fact, God clearly shows that He is the One Who saves the soul. The church at Corinth was responsible for some people getting saved; however, some were saying they were of Apollos, and others were saying they were of Paul. It was a mess! God settled the argument through the Apostle Paul in 1 Corinthians 3:7 by saying, *"So then neither is he that planteth any thing, neither he that watereth; but God that giveth the increase."* Notice, it is God's job to give the increase, not yours.

Christian, there is no pressure on you to make the perfect delivery of the Gospel, the pressure is on the Holy Ghost to take what you presented and help the person hearing the Gospel to understand it. You have to realize that God has already prepared the hearts of individuals whom He leads across your path.

I like to illustrate soul winning like a paperboy delivering the daily newspaper. The paperboy doesn't write the paper or print it; he just delivers it. The pressure is not on him to make people read the paper. Sometimes when the paperboy throws the paper, he does an excellent job and gets it right to the doorstep.

There are other times when his throw isn't the best, but the customer still gets the paper and reads the articles that were put into the paper.

A soul winner is God's paperboy. If you just deliver the Gospel, He will prepare the hearts of the individuals who hear it. God prepared the heart of the Ethiopian eunuch for Philip to give the Gospel, and He will prepare the hearts of those divine appointments whom He leads across your path. If you just deliver the Gospel the best way you know how, the Holy Spirit will take what you say and allow it to work in the hearts of those hearing it so they will accept Christ. All you have to do is just deliver it. You will find that when you take the pressure off yourself and just deliver the paper that you will run across many people whom God has already prepared.

I was sitting in a restaurant in Pennsylvania with my nephew and another pastor, when I handed a tract to our waitress and asked her to read it. I noticed that she seemed to spend a bit more time looking at the Gospel on the back, so I asked her, "Ma'am, I noticed that you are looking at the message on how to go to Heaven. Can I ask you, if you died right now, are you 100% sure that your past, present and future sins are all paid for?" She wasn't sure, so I took that tract and explained the verses to her. I then asked her if she would be willing to accept Christ. She began to cry and told me that she was going that afternoon to the wake of her friend who was killed by a stray bullet. She told me that she had been thinking about how to get to Heaven the whole morning. Right there at our table, Katie received Christ as her Saviour. There wasn't any pressure on me because the Holy Spirit had already prepared her heart for me to give the Gospel.

I was in another restaurant with a pastor friend in Iowa when I handed the waitress a Gospel tract. After going through the Gospel with her she asked, "What do I have to do to get saved?" Megan bowed her head that afternoon and received Christ as her Saviour right there in the restaurant. My friend, there are numerous stories like these that I could tell, but the only reason I'm able to tell these stories is because I realized my job is to simply give the Gospel; there's no pressure on me to be sure they get saved.

There are many plans teaching how to tell people how to get saved, but ultimately it comes down to the Holy Spirit of God working in their hearts. All you have to do is give the Gospel to people the best way you know how, and give them the opportunity to accept

Christ. Please realize that God rewards the soul winner who gives out the Gospel.

There are divine appointments like these that I told you about right where you are. Each soul-winning experience happened because my path crossed with someone else's by divine appointment. The only thing you must do is obey the command to present the Gospel, and let the Holy Spirit take your words to work on the heart He has already prepared.

It's That Simple

If you are saved, you know how to be a soul winner. The greatest soul-winning delivery is your personal testimony of how you got saved. Many may try to argue with you about what they believe, but one thing they cannot discount is what the LORD has done in your life. I have always found that soul winning is as easy as telling someone how you got saved.

Many people want to learn a simple step-by-step plan on how to witness to someone. I certainly don't claim that my plan is the best step-by-step plan on how to go soul winning, but it has been the plan that I have used for years, and it has worked thousands of times. I don't claim that I'm the best soul winner, but I do claim that anyone can follow the plan of how I go soul winning and do it themselves.

In the next few pages, I want to give you a mock delivery of how I witness to people. Again, if you do it differently than I do, it doesn't matter; the only thing that matters is that people hear the Gospel and have a chance to get saved. Many divine appointments will be experienced if you simply make yourself available to witness to people.

If you are going to be an effective soul winner, you are going to have to overcome any introvert tendencies and start approaching people to give them a Gospel tract. Find something that you can begin the conversation with, and then continue into presenting the Gospel thereafter. The following conversation is simply a condensed version with a made up name to give you an idea of how I go soul winning.

"Hey there, how are you doing today?"

Jim: "I'm doing fine."

"My name is Allen Domelle. I'm an evangelist from Texas."

(At this point I shake their hand and give them my personal tract.)

"May I ask what your name is?"

Jim: "My name is Jim Smith."

"Jim, it is sure good to meet you. I'm preaching a revival meeting at the Calvary Baptist Church this week, and I just wanted to invite you to come hear me preach the next couple of days. Do you go to church anywhere?

Jim: "Yes, I go to the Catholic church across town."

"Wonderful, I'm thrilled that you go to church. Do you go regularly, or do you miss every once in awhile?"

Jim: "I go about once a month. My work schedule doesn't allow me to make it to church as often as I'd like to."

(At this point, I try to find something that we have in common. Some simple conversation breakers are the weather, children, place of employment, or anything obvious that caused you to talk to them. I'm going to assume Jim is walking his dog.)

"Jim, that is a beautiful dog you have there. I have a couple of Rottweiler's at my house. It seems as if your dog is very well behaved."

Jim: "I've worked with my dog a bit. It does pretty good."

"Just seeing your dog makes me want to go home and take a walk with mine. Jim, I'm a preacher. My job is to be sure that every soul is set for Heaven. Jim, I would like to ask you, if you died right now, are you 100% sure that your past, present and future sins are all paid for, or do you wonder about that at times?"

Jim: "You know, there are times I wonder what would happen if I died."

"Jim, God doesn't want you to wonder. He has given us a clear plan in the Scriptures that shows us how we can be 100% sure that our sins are paid for so that we can go to Heaven."

(At this point, I pull out my New Testament without asking, or I take the tract if I don't have my New Testament and use the Gospel printed on the back.)

"Jim, Romans 3:10 says, *'As it is written, There is none righteous, no, not one:'* When God says that there is *'none righteous,'* He is saying that there is nobody who is perfect. Jim, are you perfect?"

Jim: "No, I'm not."

"Jim, on a scale from 1 to 10, 10 being perfect, and 1 being real bad, where would you put yourself on that scale?"

Jim: "I would say that I'm probably about a 7."

"Jim, the average I get when I ask people this question is about 5 to 7. Everybody knows they can't say they are a 10, and nobody wants to think that they are a 0, so they compare themselves to others and say that they are a 5 to 7. However, when you compare yourself to God, where do you truly fall on this scale?"

Jim: "Probably a 0."

"You are absolutely correct. The reason we are a 0 is because God is righteous, and we are not. God shows us that we are sinners in Romans 3:23 where it says, *'For all have sinned, and come short of the glory of God;'* Sin is breaking the laws of God. Anytime you break a law, you have to pay for it. If I were speeding down the street, the police would give me a what?"

Jim: "They would give you a ticket."

"If I robbed a bank, where would they send me?"

Jim: "They would send you to jail."

"You're absolutely correct. The reason they would do that is because I broke the law. Verse 23 says, *'all have sinned.'* That means that you have broken God's laws. God shows us what happens when we break His laws in Romans 6:23 where it says, *'For the wages of sin is death...'* Jim, let me stop right here and I will get to the rest of the verse in a second. God says that the wage for sinning is death. Jim, behind these bodies that we see is a soul that never dies. Your soul will either go to Heaven or Hell. God says that those who choose to pay for their sins themselves must die, and this death is in Hell. God also shows us what type of people end up in Hell in Revelation 21:8 where He says, *'But the fearful, and unbelieving, and the abominable, and murderers, and whoremongers, and sorcerers, and idolaters, and all liars, shall have their part in the lake which burneth with fire and brimstone: which is the second death.'* This is a pretty bad list of people, and most likely you are not most of these in this list; however, there is one type of person in this list that I have found everyone falls under. Did you see it?"

Jim: "Yes, liars."

"Jim, let me ask you, have you ever told a lie?"

Jim: "Yes."

"Jim, how many lies do you have to tell to be a liar?"

Jim: "I guess one."

"You're right. Let me ask you, how times does a person have to kill someone to be a murderer?"

Jim: "One."

"And how many times does a person have to rob a bank to be a thief?"

Jim: "One."

"Then Jim, how many times do we have to lie to be a liar?

Jim: "One."

"That's right! That means you are a liar, and according to this verse, where would you go if you died?"

Jim: "I would go to Hell."

(If you can get them to say this on their own, and they will, you will find it is easy from this point to get them to make a decision for Christ.)

"Jim, that is bad news. The good news is that God didn't leave us without help. Let me go back to Romans 6:23 where it says, *'For the wages of sin is death; but the gift of God is eternal life through Jesus Christ our Lord.'* Jim, there are two key words in this verse. The first key word is *'wages,'* and the second one is *'gift.'* A wage is something you earn, but a gift is something you freely receive, because someone else pays for it. God says that His gift is *'eternal life.'* Where do you think this eternal life is?"

Jim: "I guess Heaven."

"That is right! We already have eternal life in Hell, we don't need that twice; but, God says that He will give us eternal life in Heaven, but the only way to get it is *'through Jesus Christ.'* Jim the reason that Jesus Christ is the only One Who can give us eternal life is because He is the only One Who paid the wages for sin. Notice that the *'wages of sin is death.'* Someone still has to die for our sin if we are going to go to Heaven.

Romans 5:8 shows us, *'But God commendeth his love toward us, in that, while we were yet sinners, Christ died for us.'* Jim, God loved you so much that He was willing to leave Heaven and come to this Earth to die for your sins. He never sinned one time, but He chose to give His life for you. Jim, we could change a few words in this verse and it would mean the same thing. Look at this! *'But God commendeth his love'* towards Jim, *'in that, while'* Jim was yet a sinner, *'Christ died'* for Jim. Jim, that is exactly what this verse means. If you were the only one who sinned, Jesus would have left Heaven to die, be buried, and rise again just so that your sins could be paid.

Jim, God said in Romans 6:23 that this is a *'gift.'* In order for a gift to be yours, all you have to do is receive it. Let me show you how you receive this gift.

Romans 10:13 says, *'For whosoever shall call upon the name of the Lord shall be saved.'* The word *'whosoever'* means what?"

Jim: "I think it means anybody."

"That is right! In other words, it includes you. Let's look at this verse a little differently. *'For'* if Jim *'shall call upon the name of the Lord,'* Jim *'shall be saved.'* Jim putting your name in this verse doesn't change the meaning of this verse, because you are a *'whosever.'* God says all you have to do is realize that you are a sinner, that you can't save yourself, and that Jesus is the only One Who can pay for your sin. There must come a time when you go to Christ and call on Him through prayer and ask Him to be your Saviour. Jim, if Jesus Christ would be willing to save you right now just like you are, would you be willing to ask Him to save you?"

Jim: "Yes, I would."

"Then Jim, why don't you bow your head and say this to Christ. Please understand that just repeating a few words is not going to save you; but if you make these words your heart's prayer to Jesus, He will save you. Jim, just say this to Christ and mean it with all of your heart."

(At this point, I have them repeat out loud after me, phrase by phrase, so I can hear them. My hearing them doesn't make them get saved, but it helps me to know if they understand and are willing to get saved.)

"Jim, just say this, 'Dear Jesus, I know that I am a sinner. I know because I have sinned, I deserve Hell; but I don't want to go there. So, right now Jesus, I accept your payment on the cross, and the blood that you shed to be the payment for my sins. Come into my heart and save me, and take me to Heaven when I die. Thank you for saving me, Jesus. Amen!' Jim, did you mean that prayer when you prayed it?"

Jim: "Yes, I did!"

"Jim, if you meant it, would you shake my hand?"

(At this point, I put my hand out for them to shake it.)

"Jim, that's wonderful! Let me ask you, if you would have died fifteen minutes ago, where would you have gone?"

Jim: "I would have gone to Hell."

"And if you died right now, where would you go?"

Jim: "I would go to Heaven."

"That's right! So, how long are you saved for."

Jim: "I guess forever."

"You're right. God promised to give us 'eternal life.' He didn't say, 'Conditional life,' but He said, 'eternal life.' Jim, eternal life never ends. When Jesus paid for your sins, he paid for your past, present and future sins. That means that you are saved forever. Jim, I'm so glad that you got this settled today."

After they get saved, I do spend a little time giving them assurance of their salvation. This is so important so that they don't doubt what happened. This is also a good time to get them committed to come to church. Don't just leave them after they get saved. Close it right by giving assurance and getting them to commit to come to church and be baptized.

Soul winning is truly this simple. Today, you can take this dialogue and start showing people how to go to Heaven. Divine appointments are awaiting you if you will simply talk to people about their soul.

The Soul-Winner's Toolbox

Every trade has a toolbox. When I worked in construction, every person had a pencil, hammer, ruler, razor knife and nails. These were some of the tools we used in our trade. A physician will have a stethoscope. A seamstress will have a needle and scissors. A surgeon will have a scalpel. A secretary will have a pen and paper. A preacher will have a Bible. We could go on and on through many trades. No doubt, whatever field you are employed in has required tools to accomplish the work.

Likewise, a soul winner must have tools in their toolbox if they are going to be successful in reaching the lost for Jesus Christ and finding those divine appointments that God has scheduled for their life. The list below may not cover every tool that a soul winner needs, but it will cover the necessary ones you must have if you want to be a successful soul winner.

1. Tracts

Every Christian should carry tracts on them. There have been hundreds of times when I have been able to lead a person to Christ because I carried a tract on my person. Certainly, you can witness without a tract, but it is much easier to have a tract with you at all times to hand to someone just to break the ice. I have found that handing them my personal tract has opened the door to many conversations. I know you are not an evangelist, but most people will look at a sharp church tract when it is handed to them.

Moreover, let's say you lead someone to Christ; what are you going to leave with them so they will have some information as to where they can go to church or call for more information? Don't be found guilty of not carrying tracts with you everywhere you go. Tracts are one of the basic tools every soul winner must have.

2. New Testament

The New Testament is God's Word. It is important for people to see God's Word for themselves. It is not that you are not honest, but when they see the words of the Gospel themselves it carries more authority than just quoting the words. Hebrews 4:12 says, *"For the word of God is quick, and powerful..."* When you can point out the verses to the person whom you are trying to lead to Christ, it has more authority because it is God's Word. Certainly, you could carry a whole

Bible with you, but most people will shy away from the person carrying it. A New Testament can be put in a man's back pants pocket, inside his suit coat pocket, or a lady's purse very easily. Find yourself a New Testament where the size of the print is large enough so that most people can read it.

3. Breath mints

There is nothing worse than talking to someone whose breath makes you step back. Always be sure to take a mint just before you start soul winning. People don't want to smell the meal you had earlier in the day or your coffee breath. Be very conscious of your breath. Don't let the Devil give them any excuse to use to get away from you. Sucking on a simple breath mint just may keep someone from stepping away from hearing the most important news that will change their life forever.

4. Pen and 3x5 card

Your goal is to see someone saved, but once they get saved you need their information so you can follow up on them. I was soul winning with a gentleman years ago who would lead people to Christ but never get their names or addresses. I politely told this man that these are babies in Christ who need to be nurtured in the ways of Christ. When a baby is born, the mother doesn't leave the baby to make it on their own; rather, that mother takes that baby home and nurtures and feeds the baby until it grows up into an adult. According to 1 Corinthians 3:1, new Christians are *"babes in Christ."*

Carrying a pen and 3x5 card with you will enable you to get their information so that you can follow up on them in the weeks to come. You need to be sure to get their full name, address, age, and phone number if possible. This information can be handed to the church so that a Sunday school teacher and church staff member can follow up on that new Christian along with you.

5. Kindness

Ephesians 4:32 says, *"And be ye kind one to another..."* Learn how to be kind to people to whom you talk. There is no place in soul winning for you to be insulting or rude to a person because they don't want to listen to your presentation of the Gospel. You must realize that you may be the one who sows the seed in their heart so that another can reach them.

Several years ago I went soul winning with Evangelist Jim Lyons. I recall as we were knocking on doors that a person we talked to was very rude to us, but I watched Bro. Lyons be kind to the person in spite of their belligerent attitude. When we walked away he said to me, "Bro. Domelle, always leave every person with a good taste." He said, "There is someone who will have to talk to that person after you leave them, and you want them to have a good taste of Christians so that the next person might be able to lead them to Christ." These were golden words to me as a young man. I have always tried to follow the advice, and it has helped others to be able to reach someone for Christ whom I was not able to reach.

6. Follow-up list

It is very important that you have some way to record the names of those you lead to Christ so that you can continue to follow up on them. Just because you led someone to Christ doesn't mean you are done. Part of the Great Commission is *"baptizing them,"* and *"teaching them."* Yes, leading them to Christ is important, but a good follow-up list will help you to stay in touch with them so that you can get them to church.

7. Prayer

Every day you should pray for God to lead you to that divine appointment that He has scheduled for you. You should also pray that God would prepare your heart for them and their heart to meet you. Psalm 126:6 says, *"He that goeth forth and weepeth, bearing precious seed, shall doubtless come again with rejoicing, bringing his sheaves with him."* Don't be guilty of trying to go soul winning alone. Always ask God to help you daily to find the person whom He wants you to talk to about their eternity.

8. Draw a map

If you are a new soul winner, drawing a map in your New Testament will help you to go from one verse to the next. You know that you are going to start out in Romans 3:10, so put the ribbon of your New Testament on that page. Beside each verse, write the passage that you will go to next. This will help you to stay on track and not lose your place. I have also found it beneficial to highlight each verse in pink. It allows the person to see the verse more clearly, and it draws your eyes quickly to the place where you need to go without looking like you are unprepared.

9. Ice-breaker conversation starters

For many people, having a way to start a conversation is no easy task. They are not natural conversationalist, so striking up a conversation with someone is difficult. I have found several, what I like to call, generic conversation ice-breakers. The key to striking up a conversation with anyone is listening and looking. If you listen closely, they may say something that you have in common with them. When you are walking up to them or are approaching their home, always look for something that can be an ice-breaker.

Some of the things that I have found to be natural ice-breakers are:

- Weather
- Children
- Employment
- House landscaping
- Pets
- Where they are from
- Sports teams

These are just some of the ice-breakers I use. If you are sensitive to the Holy Spirit, He will give you that natural ice-breaker to help you strike up a conversation with someone so that they will listen to you. Don't ever underestimate the power of the Holy Spirit working on their heart. Remember that you are simply meeting a divine appointment, which means the LORD has already prepared them to meet you because there is something you both have in common that will allow them to listen to you. Don't be afraid to talk to them.

Let me also encourage you to work on your conversation skills for the sake of reaching the lost. The better you get with talking to people you don't know, the more divine appointments Christ can schedule for you.

Following Up

The area of following up on people has probably been one of the biggest weaknesses of many soul winners. Look at what the Scriptures say about your responsibility concerning the Great Commission. Matthew 28:19-20 says, *"Go ye therefore, and teach all nations, baptizing them in the name of the Father, and of the Son, and of the Holy Ghost: Teaching them to observe all things whatsoever I have commanded you: and, lo, I am with you alway, even unto the end of the world. Amen."* These two verses show what God expects from every Christian.

We often do very well with going and telling people how to get saved, but there is more to the Great Commission than just leading people to Christ. You will notice that we are commanded to be sure that they get baptized, and are taught to *"observe all things whatsoever I have commanded you."* Narrowing down the Great Commission can be done in four phrases: win them, baptize them, train them, and send them. You have not fulfilled the Great Commission with a person until all four of these areas have been completed. Certainly, it is good that people get saved;

but wouldn't it be even better if they obeyed the LORD to the point that they became soul winners themselves? There are four things you must do to accomplish this.

1. Give assurance

After you have led someone to Christ, take the time to give them assurance that they are saved forever. Assurance will give confidence. When a new Christian has the assurance of their salvation, they will be confident and grow. Hebrews 10:22 shows this truth when it says, *"Let us draw near with a true heart in full assurance of faith, having our hearts sprinkled from an evil conscience, and our bodies washed with pure water."* When a new Christian has the assurance of their salvation, they will want to put aside the things that will keep them from growing.

There are two passage of Scriptures that I use to help people understand that once they are saved they are always saved. The first verse I use is Romans 6:23. Let me go back to my conversation with Jim to show you how I would help someone understand eternal security.

"Jim, did you mean what you just prayed?"

Jim: "I sure did."

"Jim, fifteen minutes ago if you would have died, you would have gone where?"

Jim: "I would have gone to Hell."

"And if you died now, where would you go?

Jim: "I would go to Heaven."

"Why?"

Jim: "Because I asked Jesus to save me."

"You're exactly right. Jim, Romans 6:23 says that God gave you *eternal life.* God didn't say, 'conditional life,' but He said, *'eternal life.'* Let me ask you, how long does eternal life last for?"

Jim: "I guess it never ends."

"You are right! But Jim, God even shows us how secure you are in Christ. John 10:28-30 says, *'And I give unto them eternal life; and they shall never perish, neither shall any man pluck them out of my hand. My Father, which gave them me, is greater than all; and no man is able to pluck them out of my Father's hand. I and my Father are one.'* Jim, when you accepted Christ as your Saviour, you were placed in Jesus' hands. Jesus says that He and the Father *'are one,'* and that *'no man is able to pluck'* you out of His hand. The words *'no man'* includes you. It doesn't matter what you do; you will always be saved."

Once you go through this with someone, don't leave them until they understand that they will always be saved. This is important so that the Devil doesn't shake their faith which will hinder their growth.

2. Baptism

You are not done yet. They now need to follow the LORD in baptism. Don't be afraid to talk to them about this, because this is all part of them growing in the LORD. I will continue my conversation with Jim to show you how to bring someone to get baptized.

"Jim, now that you are saved, the next thing God commands you to do is to get baptized. Romans 6:3-4 says, *'Know ye not, that so many of us as were baptized into Jesus Christ were baptized into his death? Therefore we are buried with him by baptism into death: that like as Christ was raised up from the dead by the glory of the Father, even so we also should walk in newness of life.'*

Jim, baptism identifies you with Jesus Christ. I have a ring on my finger that shows that I am married. This ring doesn't make me married, but it simply tells others that I am taken and that I identify with my wife. It tells others that I am not ashamed of my wife.

Baptism does that for the Christian. According to the verses we just read, baptism is a picture of the death, burial and resurrection of Jesus Christ. When you get baptized, you will go into the water. As you stand in the water, that pictures Jesus hanging on the cross. When you go under the water, that pictures Jesus being buried. When you come up out of the water, that pictures Jesus rising again, and that tells everybody that you are going to start living a new life in Jesus Christ.

Jim, do you see the importance of being baptized?"

Jim: "Yes, but I've already been baptized."

"I understand that, but baptism comes after you get saved. Putting a wedding ring on before you get married doesn't mean anything. Likewise, getting baptized before you got saved didn't mean anything. There was a man in the Scriptures who wanted to get baptized before he got saved. He said in Acts 8:36, *'See, here is water; what doth hinder me to be baptized?'* Philip said in the next verse, *'...If thou believest with all thine heart, thou mayest. And he answered and said, I believe that Jesus Christ is the Son of God. And he commanded the chariot to stand still: and they went down both into the water, both Philip and the eunuch; and he baptized him.'* You will notice that it was only after he got saved that he was to be baptized. Jim, when did you get saved?"

Jim: "Just a few minutes ago."

"Then doesn't that mean that you should get baptized now that you are saved?"

Jim: "Yes, it does."

Of course, it may take a bit more explaining of the Scriptures to show them the need of getting baptized after they get saved, but this should help you at this point.

3. Importance of church

Once you show them they need to get baptized; it is now time to get them to commit to come to church. The best way to do this is to use their excitement about being saved to get them to tell someone else. Let me use my conversation with Jim to show you what I do to try to get people to commit to coming to church.

"Jim, are you ashamed that you got saved?"

Jim: "No, of course not."

"Jim, the Scriptures say in Romans 10:11, *'For the scripture saith, Whosoever believeth on him shall not be ashamed.'* Now that you are saved, you should tell someone about it. There are many ways you could do this. The first way could be to run up and down the street telling people you just got saved. If you did that, they would think you are crazy. You could also pay for an advertisement to tell everybody, but again that would be expensive.

The best way I have found for people to tell others about their salvation is at church. You can come to church, and I will help you tell others that you got saved. You won't have to say anything. What will happen is that I will take you up to the pastor and tell him you got saved. He will then have someone write your name down so that he can read it to the church. When your name is read to our church, the people of our church will be excited for you. Jim, how about letting me come by this Sunday to pick you up and bring you to church?"

Jim: "I can drive myself."

"I know you can, but I have found that if you come with me, I can show you where everything is in the church so you don't feel out of place. Jim, can I get you to promise the LORD that you will come with me this Sunday to church?"

Jim: "Yes, I will do that."

"Wonderful, then let's pray right now and promise the LORD that you will come."

At this point, help them word a prayer that they will promise to come with you on Sunday. I know this dialogue makes it sound easier than it actually is, but it gives you an idea of what you need to do to get them to come. It is also very important that you go by to pick them up. When you knock on their door to pick them up, it shows them your commitment to being sure that they grow in the LORD.

4. Don't ever stop following up.

Your follow-up list is going to help you to continue to follow up on your converts. Let me encourage you to never give up on anyone. Your convert may not come the first week, even after they have promised they would; however, don't give up that easily. They are a babe in Christ, and they need to see that you care for them as they grow in the LORD. I would suggest that you go by their house weekly for the next four weeks. If they don't come within that period, I would then start going every other week. I am never going to stop trying to get someone to church until they come. Church is where they are going to be introduced to their new family, and where they will be spiritually fed. I would keep visiting them periodically until they tell me that they are not interested in coming.

My friend, let me close this manuscript by simply saying that there are many divine appointments scheduled for you. Even as I was writing this last chapter, I was interrupted by the maid. After she cleaned my room, I was able to give her the Gospel, and Shanda trusted Christ as her Saviour. Come to find out, her father had a stroke two days prior to our meeting, and her heart has been heavy with concern for her father. God has divine appointments scheduled for you. I hope this manuscript will help you to meet them, and to fulfill the purpose of why God set up these appointments: seeing them saved, and following up with their growth through baptism, faithfulness to church, and culminating in them becoming soul winners. My prayer is that you will find the same joy I have received in finding divine appointments.